Red Flags

Recognizing Abuse

In Couple

Relationships

Lorene D'Adam

Copyright © 2015 Lorene D'Adam

All rights reserved.

ISBN:1518721486
ISBN-13: 978-1518721489

Dedication

With heartfelt gratitude I would like to dedicate this book to those who work and volunteer in domestic violence prevention, dating violence prevention, and crisis intervention. Your work not only raises awareness—it saves lives.

Profits from the sale of this book will be donated to dating violence prevention and domestic violence prevention programs.

Throughout this book I used he/she, him/her, and himself/herself to be gender neutral because members of both genders can be abusive just as members of both genders can be victims. Statistics at the back of this book (p.79) provide more information by gender.

Parts of this book begin with a section *in italics* intended to provide a more personal glimpse of my experience with an abusive partner. Mine is just one story. No two people have the same experience. However, you may note similarities between my story and yours or someone else's.

About the Author

Without warning, I felt the jarring impact of a blow to the left side of my head. The impact ruptured my left eardrum, rendering me instantly deaf in that ear. It was so startling that my mind seemed slow in sorting out exactly what had happened. But adrenaline asks questions later. It took over, readying me for the fight of my life. In a split second, my uncertainty switched to rage.

It was a surprisingly short trip from heaven to hell when I married a very handsome and charming man who turned out to be abusive. One price of that fateful choice? The stress of sharing parenting responsibilities with the same person I filed a restraining order against. Migraines and depression chased me for years as I tried to put together a life out of pieces so angrily ripped apart. Luckily my eardrum healed both times it was broken. But studies are confirming that domestic violence has a long half-life, leaving victims with higher-than-average incidences of chronic health problems. These problems are the result of not just physical abuse, but also the stress and adrenal fatigue that accompanies prolonged exposure to a perceived threat.[1]

As detrimental as life with an abuser was for me, what I regret even more are the negative consequences my son endured as a result of my uninformed choice.

I was naïve. I knew nothing about abuse. My parents had made marriage look easy. They trusted and respected each other and were quite a team. I left home assuming I would one day meet my soul mate—my Prince Charming—and begin a relationship as loving as the one my parents shared.

When an irresistible man with a great sense of humor appeared one day and swept me into his whirlwind of passion, I believed we were starting a wonderful life together. I was in love. What could possibly go wrong?

Upon his urging, I married him much too quickly and

too soon after a death in my immediate family. I trusted my husband before he proved himself to be trustworthy. Filled with optimism, I quit a good job and moved far away with him, all the while thinking I was clear-eyed and aware.

The abuse started gradually, in private. I didn't recognize it as abuse. As quickly as the red flags appeared, I tried to dismiss them, rather than identify them as helpful warnings. They clashed with my picture-perfect life.

There were half-joking insults that caused me to question something I had said or the value of things I had always enjoyed. There were discrepancies in details that made me question my memory rather than wonder about his honesty. I caught him spying on me, but of course he denied it.

This was not the blissful relationship I had envisioned. But I had taken vows, and I intended to be part of a successful marriage. I subdued a growing sense of discomfort with the hope that my husband would change. Everyone else thought he was a great guy. All they saw was that likable, charming man I fell in love with.

But a monstrous nightmare began when the abuse became physical. I was stunned by it. The adrenaline surge I felt was unlike anything I had ever experienced before. And when the physical abuse began, I was a few weeks pregnant.

My husband's immediate remorse seemed sincere. He tried to convince me it would never happen again. But when I was eight months pregnant it *did* happen again.

A month later my son was born. I returned to work when he was fifteen months old. As luck would have it, I found a job with an organization dedicated to domestic violence prevention and crisis intervention. There I learned things about abuse I wished I had known years before. I met survivors of abuse who could finally speak openly about what they had endured. I discovered that the problem of domestic violence is far worse and more widespread than I had imagined. Through counseling, I identified misconceptions I held about relationships and learned problem-solving and limit-setting skills. I found the support I needed to leave a doomed marriage and move on.

But still today, the statistics concerning dating violence and domestic violence are persistently high, and over the years I have met far too many victims of abuse.

I've written this book because I want you to recognize the reds flags of abuse earlier than I did. I want you to heed the cues I ignored. I want you to have a keener sense than I did of what makes a relationship healthy.

If you are currently involved with an abusive partner, I want to shine a light of support and encouragement on the path toward a better life, free of abuse.

What happened to me and to so many other victims of abuse doesn't have to happen to you.

Contents

Introduction	1
PART I: The Healthy Stuff	5
Boundaries	7
Trust	17
Respect	21
PART II: Things to Consider	23
Could You Become a Victim of Abuse?	25
Those First Red Flags	33
PART III: The Unhealthy Stuff	37
Types of Abuse	39
Verbal, Emotional, Psychological	42
Digital	45
Financial	48
Physical	51
Sexual	54
Spiritual	56
The Cycle of Abuse	57
PART IV: Leaving Abuse Behind	63
Why Doesn't the Victim Leave?	65
How to Break Up	73
Being Single	75
Conclusion	77
Resources & Sources	79
Acknowledgements	93

Introduction

Red Flag: An uncomfortable but important gut feeling that something is wrong, a warning signal.

Is someone abusing you or a loved one? Are you witnessing behaviors that make you wonder how healthy the relationship is? Are reds flags popping up?

Abuse can occur no matter your education level, ethnicity, gender identity, sexual preference, or socioeconomic status. Anyone can be abusive. Anyone can be a victim of abuse.

Humans are relational beings. We long for connection. But do two people simply meet, fall in love, and live happily ever after? If only it were that simple.

Courtrooms are crowded with people seeking divorces and restraining orders. There are trials with assault and even murder charges involving people who once were in love. Clearly, too many people choose the wrong partner, and tragically some stay too long in abusive relationships.

If you grew up around abusive behaviors, you might think these behaviors are normal and acceptable. If you grew up in a relatively peaceful home, like I did, you might be too trusting and naïve about abuse.

Behind Closed Doors

This is where most abuse happens. It's awful. It destroys relationships. It hurts families. It robs people of their self-esteem, power, health, happiness, and peace of mind. It can even cost a victim his/her life. Feelings of embarrassment, guilt, shame, and fear can accompany abuse. Asking someone about the abuse he/she endured can trigger painful flashbacks and post-traumatic stress. It's not the typical kitchen-table topic. But if we intend to put a stop to abuse, we have to understand more about the victim, the abuser, and the misuse of power and control.

This book provides a brief overview of both healthy and unhealthy behaviors in relationships. It explains the importance of boundaries, trust, and respect. It alerts you to situations that could make you more vulnerable to abuse. It offers reasons why people ignore red flags, gives examples of abuse, describes the cycle of abuse, provides suggestions for victims who are still with abusive partners, and offers tips for safely breaking up with an unhealthy partner. Let's get better at spotting abuse, so we will know exactly what to do if those red flags appear.

National Domestic Violence Hotline:

1-800-799-SAFE (7233)

TTY: 1-800-787-3224

www.thehotline.org

This hotline is free, confidential, and operates 24 hours a day, every day. Trained personnel can answer questions and also refer you to help in your area. Online Chat: 7:00 a.m. – 2:00 a.m. central time

Teen & Young Adult Confidential Helpline:

1-866-331-9474

www.loveisrespect.org

Online Chat: 24/7/365

Text: loveis to 22522

If while reading this book you discover that you are abusive, help is available. Call the hotline.

PART I

The Healthy Stuff

> Boundaries
> Trust
> Respect

Boundaries

I had little independence when he was in town. I mistook all the attention for caring, not controlling—at least at first. I had the same reaction to his excessive phone calls when he was out of town. I assumed it was part of the honeymoon phase—that time when you are so crazy in love that you hardly let your new partner out of your sight.

Individuals grow up in environments that, for better or worse, influence their ideas about how relationships should work. Communication skills, problem-solving skills, and limit-setting skills are sometimes lacking. But **healthy people form partnerships** hoping to influence each other in positive and supportive ways.

A certain amount of give and take is required as partners recognize their influence, share power, and learn how to express themselves and navigate conflicts. Every relationship requires work. When problems arise, healthy partners work together toward a solution that is fair for both people. If they disagree about too many things, too often, they may decide they are not compatible and choose to go separate ways. It might be disappointing, but at least it is safe.

An abusive partner lacks understanding or doesn't care about the cooperation and compromise necessary for a healthy relationship. Instead, he/she wants **power and control** over you and will try to weaken your self-esteem by undermining your strengths and magnifying your real (or invented) weaknesses. He/she may be very jealous and possessive and may try to isolate you from the people and things you love.

These are **red flags.** They are unhealthy attempts to control you. Speaking up about unfair treatment or deciding to leave an abusive partner can spark an angry, scary, harmful response—another **red flag**.

But you can't always tell at the beginning of a relationship whether you have chosen a healthy or an unhealthy partner. Both people may be on their best behavior, and everything seems great. This is why setting boundaries is a good idea.

Boundaries are the necessary limits you set to protect aspects of your life that matter. As a child, it was your parents' responsibility to be on the lookout for people or things that could harm you. It was their job to provide boundaries to keep you safe. Hopefully, they did their job. But as adults, it is up to each of us to protect ourselves.

In the process of establishing boundaries you think about what matters to you, how you wish to be treated, and what you will or won't tolerate. Because you take a proactive approach to your own well-being, you notice when someone disrespects you or doesn't meet your standards. So you reduce your chances of being redefined or controlled by an abusive person.

Take a good look at yourself. What makes you who you are? What makes you happy?

Focus on:

- Your strengths
- Your favorite hobbies or activities
- How you wish to be treated
- The people and things you value in your life
- The things you hope to accomplish

When it comes to your happiness, all of these things matter. They provide joy, support, and security. They keep your life interesting and on track. Sometimes we take them for granted. But it's important to be mindful of them, because if you have no boundaries and you pick the wrong partner, you can lose what matters to you.

Without boundaries, you can be pressured to do things you otherwise would not do. You might stop spending time with people or activities you used to enjoy. You might say **yes** when you would rather say **no**. You could wind up doing too much for someone while consistently getting less in return. You could become entangled in too much negative drama and even believe you deserve it. The downhill slide might be gradual enough that you don't notice just how unhappy or frustrated you have become.

Here are several examples of boundaries along with how someone might communicate them. As you read these, consider what boundaries will work for you and how you might express them to your partner.

How quickly your relationship moves toward commitment or intimacy:

- "I need to slow our relationship down. I need more time to get to know you better."
- "I have other goals before getting married and having kids."

How often you wish to be contacted by phone, text, or email:

- "Except for emergencies, don't call or text me at work."
- "I need to study tonight, so please don't call me."

What you require regarding privacy:

- "Don't sneak up on me."

- "Don't read my journal, my personal emails, or my personal text messages."

What personal property you are willing or not willing to share:

- "This has sentimental value. I don't share it."

- "You may borrow my car, but replace the gas you use."

How much you are willing to share financially:

- "I'll pay for this meal if you pay for the next."

- "I'm saving my money for school, so I can't lend you money."

Your preferences regarding affection and intimacy:

- "I won't risk having unprotected sex."

- "I'm uncomfortable with certain public displays of affection."

The time you need to enjoy family, friends, or personal interests:

- "My cousins and I never miss this tradition."
- "I have one practice and one game each week."

How your partner speaks to you:

- "Don't disrespect me."
- "Please don't use those words around me."

Having boundaries is a good start. But, implementing them can be challenging. If you are not used to being assertive you might instead become defensive or apologetic. You might worry about the consequences of speaking up for yourself.

It takes practice, courage, and belief in yourself to speak up. If someone treats you in a way that you dislike, it is up to you to say, **"That is not okay."**

If a new situation arises and you have no boundary for it, you can buy some time by saying, **"I need time to consider how I feel about this."** Then you can decide on a boundary that will work for you.

Standing up for yourself may feel awkward at first, but with practice it will become easier. It's important to know your limits and be assertive when necessary. Don't forget: **You are the guardian of your happiness and security**.

Draw the Line | Respect the Line

After making your boundaries known, if someone disrespects them, that is a **red flag**. He/she is not ready to be a healthy partner. Step back and hold others accountable for their behavior. Don't waste time in a relationship with someone who cannot respect your boundaries.

It is not your responsibility to change others, only to decide what is acceptable in your own life. But sometimes a compassionate person with good intentions feels pity for an abuser who has a less fortunate background. The victim earnestly wants to help and believes it is possible to change the abuser.

Adverse Childhood Experiences

Many perpetrators of abuse have experienced childhood adversity that has far-reaching, negative consequences. The effects are not easily overcome and certainly cannot be fixed by a well-intentioned partner.

The ACE Study[2] presents evidence of how *Adverse Childhood Experiences* lead to health, social, and economic risks. You can find your ACE score and that of your partner by using an ACE score calculator at **www.acestudy.org**.

Meanwhile, the effect of abuse on a victim and on any children who witness the abuse can cause more harm. Abuse has a profound impact on children who witness it.[3] It may even affect unborn children.[4]

Don't think you can fix someone else. Unfortunately, you *cannot* fix someone else.

When it comes to boundaries, one size does not fit all. You can have certain boundaries with people you know and trust and different boundaries with others who are less familiar to you or less trustworthy. A boundary can change if and when *you* decide to change it.

Boundaries can prevent you from losing what matters to you and from being mistreated by a controlling partner. Establishing boundaries will help you feel happier, safer, and more comfortable.

1-800-799-7233 www.thehotline.org
1-866-331-9474 www.loveisrespect.org

Trust

A wave of skepticism washed over me. I felt sick. I quietly made a mental inventory of every detail I thought I knew about my husband. He was new to the city when we met. The few friends he had were actually just co-workers. There was no one who could provide an informal background check. Until now, it had never crossed my mind that he might be a liar. But too many things were not adding up. I silenced my skeptical thoughts. My husband had to be trustworthy. The alternative—that he would lie about insignificant as well as significant things—was too dreadful to ponder this early in my marriage.

Trust is precious and fragile. It is an essential element of every healthy relationship. It builds slowly but can vanish in an instant. Trust building is a layered process that needs a strong foundation. You and your partner must earn each other's trust. You must each prove that you are trustworthy.

It takes time to really get to know someone. Trust can only build as you observe consistently trustworthy behaviors over time. Early in the relationship, both of you are on your best behavior. You haven't seen each other at your worst. But a person's true nature will surface, given enough time.

A layer of trust is added each time someone treats you with respect, cares about how you are feeling, listens, and proves to be reliable and truthful.

If someone disregards your feelings, shares your secrets with others, belittles you, lies, or is unreliable pay attention. Those are **red flags.** That person is violating your trust, not building it. Many relationships fail because trust has been violated and cannot be restored.

Strive to be trustworthy, and don't continue to invest time in a relationship with someone who has proven unable or unwilling to earn your trust.

Unearned Trust

When you decide to trust a person before he/she proves to be trustworthy, you place yourself at risk. If you grew up around trustworthy people, you may assume most people are trustworthy. But extending trust that has not been earned may cost you. Be more cautious.

There is a Russian proverb, "Trust, but verify." It means that even if a person seems reliable, do more investigation. Take care of yourself. Let others earn your trust.

Respect

I felt isolated after only a year of marriage. We had moved far away from my family. New people we met were nice. But we had stopped socializing with others, partly because my husband was unpredictable. His anger and rudeness might suddenly erupt in public as it had, too often, in private. My respect for him was dwindling, but I still wanted others to think he was respectable.

Respect is another essential element of a healthy relationship. Respectful partners hold each other in high regard and treat each other fairly. They share power as they support each other's goals and interests. They honor each other's boundaries and protect each other's reputations.

When it comes to communication, respectful partners value each other's opinions. They tell the truth. They are not afraid to express their feelings or thoughts. They listen well. They keep each other's private information private.

When it comes to conflicts, respectful partners keep disagreements civil, manage their anger, exercise patience and forgiveness, and show a readiness to resolve misunderstandings.

Respectful partners treat each other the way they want to be treated. They feel safe with each other and have no fear of harm.

Does this describe your relationship? If not, do you recognize the **red flags**?

Boundaries, trust, and respect are related. When both individuals know their boundaries, honor each other's boundaries, and trust and respect each other, a healthy partnership can grow.

PART II

Things to Consider

Could You Become a Victim of Abuse?

Those First Red Flags

Could You Become a Victim of Abuse?

It was a romantic setting for a first date. Over dinner he made it quite clear that he was interested in a permanent relationship with me. He asked if I was looking for the same thing. I had never had the "I am looking for commitment" conversation on a first date. It caught me off guard. A wiser person might have laughed inwardly—because it was absurd! We hardly knew each other. But I found him so charming. I didn't laugh. In fact, that evening I lost my capacity to think clearly. I was falling in love.

In a **healthy relationship**, partners share power. Nobody is perfect, but healthy partners accept each other's imperfections while providing a supportive, safe environment for growth and improvement.

In an **unhealthy relationship**, an abusive person is not interested in sharing power. He/she is interested in gaining and maintaining power and control over his/her partner. Your imperfections are not safe with an abuser who may use any insecurity you have against you. The environment is not as supportive or safe. Growth and improvement rarely happen.

Given this contrast, why would anyone choose an unhealthy relationship? Here are possible reasons:

1. You are *in* love (or in lust.) When you are *in* love your brain chemistry actually changes, distorting reality by improving your perceptions of both the person you are *in* love with and your potential for a future together.[5] You feel a fierce loyalty to your partner that prevents you from evaluating him/her objectively. He/she is the unforgettable object of your desire. You are on an emotional quest with goals of spending more time together and deepening your commitment to each other. You may think you love the person. But loving someone and being *in* love are two different things.

Now, you may have subconsciously expected your Prince Charming (or the female equivalent) to magically appear one day. (This expectation was brought to you by the makers of fairy tales, romantic novels and movies, and love song lyrics.) It's an unrealistic expectation, but that's only part of the problem.

When brain chemistry returns to normal (because eventually it does), people say the "honeymoon" is over. That simply means the distortion is gone. Your emotions have settled down, and you are now able to see more clearly.

What you see may be an *abusive* partner. Red flags you had overlooked may now be impossible to ignore. Incompatibilities that seemed insignificant may now create constant friction. Your boundaries may be disregarded. Trust and respect may seem impossible. You might be faced with a partner you don't even *like*, let alone love.

On the other hand, once the initial excitement of the "honeymoon" phase ends, if each person still likes, trusts, and respects the other, a more stable and lasting love can grow provided both partners choose to invest in the relationship.

Love is a term that can mean different things to different people. The same goes for commitment. So in a relationship, it is important for both partners to understand each other's expectations.

Enjoy being *in* love but realize that it doesn't last. Be mindful of its inherent distortion.

2. You have low self-esteem. If you have low self-esteem an abusive person might choose you.

Low self-esteem: The negative beliefs or opinions you have about yourself that influence the way you see yourself.

You may suffer from low self-esteem:

- If you were the victim of abuse or neglect

- If you were told something was wrong with you

- If praise or affection was withheld from you

- If you felt excessive guilt or shame over something that happened

- If you failed to meet your parents' or peers' expectations

- If you were criticized or compared to someone else who always seemed better

- If you are part of any group that suffers discrimination

- If you are somehow different and made to feel like a misfit

People with low self-esteem are more likely to:

- Lack confidence

- Lack boundaries

- Be passive and submissive

- Tolerate unhealthy behavior just to have a partner

Our culture is full of advertising images, stories about celebrities, reality TV, movies, song lyrics, music videos, etc. You are bombarded with images and messages that can make you feel as if you are not good-looking enough, sexy enough, smart enough, rich enough, or adventurous enough. (Also, we see so much violence and abuse in movies, on TV, or in video games that we grow numb to it, as if it's to be expected.)

Low self-esteem is not all that uncommon. Many people struggle with some degree of low self- esteem at some point in their lives. But if low self-esteem would cause you to settle for someone who would mistreat you, take advantage of the numerous websites and books about improving self-esteem that are easy to find with a simple online search. Counseling can also help to improve your self-esteem.

3. You are feeling pressure to find a partner. There is pressure to find your special someone, as if remaining single would imply that something is wrong with you, or as if partnering is part of some success scorecard (graduate—check, get married—check).

Sometimes a person chooses a partner recklessly to escape the home he/she grew up in.

Pressure can come from family, friends, or yourself to

find someone, get married, and have children.

A new partner may pressure you to commit. It might seem flattering, but it could be a **red flag**.

If you are so uncomfortable with being single that you rush from one failed relationship to the next, with no more than a vague understanding of what went wrong with the last relationship, your chances are greater of choosing an unhealthy partner.

4. You are naïve: Even with high self-esteem, you might not immediately recognize abuse if you grew up in a home that had none. You might lack boundaries. You might be too trusting or gullible.

5. You are in shock. A big loss such as the death of someone close to you may cause shock. Shock is deceptive because you think you are making good decisions when, in fact, you are not. Shock can last well beyond a year.

Be aware of your vulnerability. Don't rush into commitment. Notice whether your partner is supportive and respectful or not. Until you are sure, don't make choices that would hinder your ability to leave such as:

- Getting pregnant
- Marrying too quickly
- Quitting your job or school
- Comingling property or financial resources
- Moving away from your support system to be with your partner
- Alienating family and friends

At the start of a new romance it's hard to imagine anything going wrong—until it does.

1-800-799-7233   www.thehotline.org
1-866-331-9474   www.loveisrespect.org

Those First Red Flags

We were talking with friends after church when the conversation turned to skydiving. "Ask him about it," I said, nodding toward my husband, "He's done some skydiving." My husband shot me a half-puzzled, half-disapproving look. "I have not," he told our friends with a tone that suggested I was in the habit of telling tall tales. I felt momentarily crazy. I dropped out of the conversation to search my memory for that unusual detail I was certain he shared on our first date. Or did I dream that?

Some survivors of abuse say they never saw the abuse coming. Others can remember an incident that should have tipped them off. At that moment, if they had decided to leave, they could have spared themselves some heartache. Instead, they chose to ignore the behavior.

If you notice a **red flag** near the start of your relationship, (for example: a hurtful remark; behavior that scares you; catching your partner in a lie; catching him/her snooping through your things; a more-than-playful, rough, physical encounter; or an unreasonable flash of anger) common sense would tell you to leave that relationship. If the relationship is just starting, it shouldn't be that difficult to leave. Except, **when you are *in* love, common sense takes a back seat.** So instead you might make excuses for the abuse, to convince yourself that it wasn't that bad or that it was even your fault.

Sometimes the abuse begins only after circumstances are more entangled making it difficult to leave. Again it might seem easier to ignore the red flag and excuse the abuser's behavior.

Why do people ignore red flags?

- It could be that you haven't experienced abuse before and you don't recognize it.

- Maybe you're hoping it's a one-time event – you'd prefer to give your partner the benefit

- Perhaps you underestimate the danger.

- It could be that you *do* realize how bad it is, but you feel stuck due to circumstances.

- Maybe you believe you can fix it.

- Perhaps you don't want to be single, so you are weighing whether you can tolerate some offensive behaviors.

- It could be that you are worried about your reputation, or you are too embarrassed to admit you picked an unhealthy partner.

- Maybe you think you deserve abuse.

The onset of abuse can be confusing. You had assumed your partner was trustworthy, respected you, and cared about you. But now you are not so sure. Maybe you are being ridiculed or insulted by your partner. Perhaps you doubt yourself because of condescending remarks your partner has made. Or you have become isolated from people and things you enjoyed. Maybe you have tried to discuss your concerns with your partner, but instead of being heard you are being blamed.

Those **red flags are warning signs**. And even though your heart might *wish* to ignore them, **pay close attention**. They are telling you that your relationship is unhealthy and possibly even unsafe. Not only that, if you ignore the red flags your partner may think you will tolerate more abuse. The best time to end an abusive relationship is when those first red flags appear.

1-800-799-7233   www.thehotline.org

1-866-331-9474   www.loveisrespect.org

PART III

The Unhealthy Stuff

Types of Abuse
The Cycle of Abuse

Types of Abuse

The six types of abuse that follow can overlap—some of the behaviors listed as one type could also be considered another type. The behaviors range from annoying to reportable to life threatening. Victims often suffer from not just one but rather several types of abuse.

Some people mistakenly think the only *real* abuse is physical abuse. But there are non-physical abusive behaviors that can be as harmful or worse.

Abuse is a strategy that employs subtle and not-so-subtle measures to gain and maintain power and control over you—by diminishing your power and your sense of self-worth, and by causing you to question what you value, how you think, or whether you could manage alone—so you will be more controllable and dependent on your partner.

There is no way to predict which abusive behavior(s) will appear, when they will start, or how quickly they might escalate. Abuse can start gradually, increasing over time or suddenly and severely.

Please note: These lists do not include every possible example of abuse. If you are experiencing a behavior that causes a red flag, but it is not on any of the following lists, it can still be abuse. Call The Hotline for further clarification. Sometimes even a conversation with someone who is trained and understands this subject can *really* help.

If the following examples include behaviors you are experiencing, then you are a victim of abuse. Realizing that you are a victim of abuse can be troubling. But it can also be motivating. You can take action to change your life, your children's lives—if children are involved—and even any pets' lives for the better. Your life and theirs may depend on it.

Ask yourself:

Is this a person I should be with?

Do I deserve this kind of treatment?

Is this love?

Now tell yourself:

No one deserves abuse.

Love never includes harmful behaviors or danger.

1-800-799-7233   www.thehotline.org

1-866-331-9474   www.loveisrespect.org

Verbal, Emotional, or Psychological Abuse

For some time now, my husband had been ridiculing me. If a total stranger had acted this way, I would have regarded it as rude. But because it came from someone who supposedly loved me and from a man I was legally bound to, I took it to heart. It had several forms such as "jokes" about my appearance or something I said, or sarcastic remarks about my housekeeping or cooking. He trivialized my hobbies and interests as silly wastes of effort, money, or time. He was thoughtful toward others while at the same time thoughtless toward me.

People sometimes underestimate the emotional and psychological harm caused by words. Words don't break bones or leave bruises on your skin. They don't send you to the emergency room. But the damage to your sense of self-worth and happiness can be severe and longer lasting than a physical injury.

Physical abuse is obvious but verbal abuse can be confusing. For example, a partner who makes condescending remarks about your intelligence, your sanity, your memory, or your emotional stability may then say that he/she was only joking and blame you for being "too sensitive." A dishonest partner can play mind games. As the abuse continues and even worsens, you might begin to doubt your own thinking and believe what your abusive partner says instead.

Red Flags of Verbal, Emotional, or Psychological Abuse:

- Name-calling, yelling, or cursing
- Embarrassing you in front of others
- Insulting, criticizing, or hurtful teasing
- Lying, and then denying the lie
- Calling you crazy or doing things to make you feel crazy
- Minimizing your feelings
- Saying you deserve abuse
- Ordering you around
- Looking or behaving in ways that scare you

- Blaming you for his/her actions
- Blackmailing you
- Telling your secrets
- Acting possessive and jealous
- Threatening you or any children or pets with physical harm
- Threatening self-harm
- Giving you the silent treatment, ignoring you, or withholding affection
- Invading your privacy
- Spying on you or stalking you
- Making you feel that no matter how hard you try, what you do or how you are, is never good enough

Digital Abuse

Please be aware: Tracking and monitoring devices can be installed in your telephone, computer, and car without your knowledge. There are resources at the back of this book (p.83) and through The Hotline that offer *technology* safety tips.

This type of abuse includes emails, texts, social media messages, phone calls, pictures sent electronically, and other behaviors. Victims are threatened, stalked, and harassed—sometimes even to the point of suicide.

If digital abuse is happening to you, keep a detailed log as evidence. Include the date, time, and number of offenses. Take screen shots or make note of any transmissions. Record threats. Document whatever you can. Don't suffer in silence. Tell the abusive person to stop and record or document that instruction. If the behavior doesn't stop, report it to the police. Seek help by calling The Hotline for referrals to help in your area and for information about filing a restraining order.

Red Flags of Digital Abuse:

- Excessive texting, emailing, or telephoning asking where you are, what you are doing, and whom you are with

- Monitoring your phone calls, emails, or social media

- Insisting on knowing your passwords, checking your computer history, phone logs, or messages

- Violating your privacy by posting embarrassing pictures or comments

- Using messages or pictures to blackmail you

- Bullying or spreading rumors about you

- Scaring you with intimidating messages

- Stalking you with tracking technology

- Sexting

Sexting involves sending nude, semi-nude, or sexually suggestive photos by cell phone or electronically. **Letting someone else possess nude or sexually suggestive pictures of you (either**

digital or analog) is a bad idea. Once they are out of your possession, you have lost control over how others may use them against you, even if you never thought they would.

Once Online - Always Online

Don't think that online pictures will easily disappear. They won't. Although you may have deleted them, they are still in existence and can be retrieved. An online search of you that includes such images could ruin your reputation and sabotage future education, housing, and employment opportunities. It can be very expensive to try to take them offline.

Please note: Check your state laws. If the picture was taken of someone under age 18, **sexting may involve three felonies:** creation of, distribution of, and possession of child pornography.

Financial Abuse

I had always paid my bills on time when I was single. But now we were living beyond our means. My husband and I agreed, or so I thought, to stop using our credit cards except to buy gasoline. Several weeks later, he gave me an expensive handbag on my birthday. It made me uneasy because it was more than we could afford. But he assured me he had been putting money aside for months and hadn't used a credit card. Just two days later the billing statement came, and there was the handbag charge.

If your partner undermines or destroys your earning potential, your credit rating, or your chances for a better education, you lose some of your financial freedom and power. If your partner controls all of the money and assets in your relationship, there is much greater potential for abuse.

Red Flags of Financial Abuse:

- Making you pay for everything or for more than your share

- Damaging or destroying your valuables and

not replacing them

- Interfering with your ability to study

- Preventing you from getting a job

- Ridiculing your plans for self-improvement

- Causing you to be late or to miss important application or testing deadlines

- Causing you to be fired by showing up at your workplace or by calling or texting excessively during work hours

- Taking your paycheck and stating that you are not smart enough to handle budgeting

- Controlling what you spend by putting you on an allowance

- Using your credit card without your permission

- Using shared credit cards excessively

- Opening charge accounts or borrowing money in your name without your knowledge by forging your signature

- Convincing you to go into debt for him/her

but not repaying the debt in a timely manner

- Belittling you for not contributing enough financially because you are at home with the children

Physical Abuse

We were in Hawaii when my husband hit me the first time. I fled our hotel room in the rental car. When I could calm down, I located a doctor to examine and treat my broken eardrum. When the doctor asked how it had happened, I was too humiliated—and too protective of my husband—to say he had assaulted me. So I lied. "My husband and I were just playing around, and he accidently hit me," I replied. After the doctor visit, I didn't know where to go. It was getting dark. Most of my things were in the hotel room, and we were scheduled to fly home the following day using my husband's airline employee passes. So I returned to the hotel. He was there. Tearfully, he apologized. He said he was very sorry for hitting me, and that it would never happen again.

I was far from home, too stunned to know what to do. I had been assaulted, and I had been ashamed enough to lie to the doctor about it. Had I known then what I know now, I would have returned to the hotel room accompanied by police. I would have gathered my things, called someone for help, and bought my ticket to a new life.

It's a horribly unexpected thing to be physically injured by your "loved one." However, it happens far too often, and usually stays hidden behind closed doors. Physical abuse can begin after verbal abuse has worn down your self-esteem.

As with other types of abuse, your partner may blame you for the incident. Or you may believe you provoked it. But **abuse is *never* the victim's fault**. If you stay in a physically abusive relationship though, you are putting yourself and any children or pets at risk of greater harm.

Red Flags of Physical Abuse:

- Hitting, slapping, punching, shoving, kicking, pulling hair, or spitting on you
- Throwing something at you or near you
- Breaking, damaging, or shattering things
- Driving recklessly
- Harming children or pets
- Threatening you with weapons
- Depriving you of sleep or food

- Abandoning you in an unsafe place
- Forcing you to drink alcohol or do drugs
- Restraining you or blocking your path
- Physically intimidating you
- Strangling you

Strangulation can kill more easily than you may realize. As few as 10 seconds of pressure on your neck's blood vessels can cause you to lose consciousness. It only takes 33 pounds of pressure to close off your windpipe (trachea). Your raging abuser could kill you in just four to five minutes with his/her bare hands.

If you survive an attempted strangulation you are still at very great risk. That is because strangulation is one of the best predictors of future homicide.[6]

If someone attempts this with you call 911 and report it to the police. You may have no visible signs of strangulation, but seek medical attention. You may have internal injuries and delayed symptoms resulting from damage to your trachea, esophagus, or larynx.

Sexual Abuse

You might be reluctant to report this type of abuse because of its intimate nature or because you fear you will be blamed. Potential consequences such as pregnancy and sexually transmitted infections (STIs) can change your life. Don't suffer alone. Call The Hotline for support.

Red Flags of Sexual Abuse:

- Forcing or threatening to use force to get you to do anything sexual you do not want to do, including involving other people or watching pornography

- Pressuring or forcing you to have unprotected sex (Proper protection can prevent STIs and unintended pregnancies.)

- Threatening to get sex elsewhere if you don't comply

- Making sexually degrading remarks or accusations about you

- Touching or groping you when you don't want it

- Assuming that your permission is no longer required since you consented to sex in the past

- Getting you drunk or high to take advantage of you, or pressuring you to use drugs or alcohol before sex

- Controlling what you wear or don't wear

- Forcing penetration without your consent—this is **Rape**.

The rapist could be someone you have just begun dating, your fiancé(e), or the partner you live with, including your spouse. It could also be a stranger, a relative, or someone you have known for some time. After this flagrant violation of your boundaries, the rapist may blame you. But abuse is *never* the victim's fault. **Rape is *never* the victim's fault**. There is specific support for all victims of rape. Call The Hotline for resources in your area.

Spiritual Abuse

Spirituality is personal. Differences involving religious beliefs, philosophies, or spirituality are compatibility issues to consider when deciding whether to commit to a partner. But certain behaviors, which can come under the guise of religion or spirituality, are abusive.

Red Flags of Spiritual Abuse:

- Controlling how you dress or behave, or being disrespectful and using his/her beliefs or quoting scripture to justify the behavior

- Ridiculing your beliefs

- Preventing you from practicing your beliefs or from meeting with others who share your beliefs

- Forcing you to practice your partner's beliefs

- Prohibiting you from using birth control when your personal beliefs do not conflict with the use of birth control

The Cycle of Abuse

Flowers and a card would always arrive after my husband's verbally abusive outbursts. These were delivered to my office, for show, never to me privately at home. It worked. My coworkers thought my husband was exceptional. Their husbands were not so thoughtful. "Aren't you the lucky one?" they would say. I wanted to tell them, "You are as fooled as I was! There is a flip side to that guy you perceive as charming and wonderful. He is an angry, abusive fraud. These flowers are nothing but a meaningless apology for behavior that does not change." But, instead, embarrassed about my pathetic predicament, I went along with their characterization.

Abusive behavior tends to cycle. Dr. Lenore Walker[7] described the "Cycle of Violence" in 1979.[8] It is also known as the "Cycle of Abuse" because an abusive outburst does not necessarily involve physical violence. With or without physical violence the cycle progresses like this:

At first, things are peaceful between you and your partner.

But then tension begins to build in the relationship causing increasing discomfort.

The buildup of tension finally releases through an explosion—an abusive outburst as your partner loses control of his/her anger.

Afterward, at least at first, your partner seems remorseful and tries to convince you that it will never happen again. He/she seems sincere and loving toward you. If this is your first go round with the cycle, you may try to dismiss the outburst as a one-time event.

Some of us have been taught to be quick to forgive when someone asks for forgiveness or for a second chance. You may decide to forgive him/her and stay in the relationship.

In fact, at first you might think the abusive outburst

was caused by something *you* did or didn't do, or something *you* said or didn't say. That is because your abuser may blame you rather than take responsibility for his/her lack of control.

The abuser might say:

"*You* made me angry."

"*You* made me lose control."

"I wouldn't have said those things or hurt you:

- if you hadn't said _____. (fill in the blank)."
- if you hadn't (done)_____. (fill in the blank)."
- if you had just done what I told you to do."

"If you really loved me you would do what I ask."

You may even try hard to prevent any future explosions. It may feel like you are walking on eggshells.

Here is what you should remember:

The responsibility lies with the abusive person to

control his/her own anger. No matter how many reasons or excuses either one of you might make for the abuse the simple truth is this: **You are never responsible for someone else's actions. If you are the victim, it is NOT your fault, and it is NOT under your control.** The only way to guarantee avoiding future explosions is to leave the relationship.

The duration of a cycle can vary. At first, the explosions may be weeks or even months apart. But as the abuse continues, here are the changes you are likely to witness:

- The time between the explosions will shorten.

- The apologies will likely disappear leaving only tension separating one abusive explosion from the next.

- The abuse will likely escalate. If it didn't start as physical abuse, it will probably become physical, and more harmful. Your abusive partner may even threaten to kill you. We hear of these homicides too often in the news.

Living with such turmoil is very stressful and can cause long-term health problems for you and your children. But leaving an abusive relationship is not as easy as one might assume. Let's take a look at some reasons why a victim might stay in an abusive relationship.

National Domestic Violence Hotline:

1-800-799-SAFE (7233)

TTY: 1-800-787-3224

www.thehotline.org

This hotline is free, confidential, and operates 24 hours a day, every day. Trained personnel can answer questions and also refer you to help in your area.

Online Chat: 7:00 a.m. – 2:00 a.m. central time

Teen & Young Adult Confidential Helpline:

1-866-331-9474

www.loveisrespect.org

Online Chat: 24/7/365

Text: loveis to 22522

If while reading this book you discover that you are abusive, help is also available to you. Call the hotline.

PART IV

Leaving Abuse Behind

Why Doesn't the Victim Leave?
How to Break Up
Being Single

Why Doesn't the Victim Leave?

The second time my husband hit me was different from the first in one way. It was no longer an anomaly. Gone was the hope that it would never happen again. His promise was meaningless. Once again, I felt my adrenaline surge. At eight months pregnant, I feared it might induce premature labor. I was a mother bear with an unborn cub to protect. "Get out!" I ordered. He hurried out the door. I set the lock behind him then sat down and wept. But later that night, my husband came home. Allowing an assailant back into my home defied common sense. But I was exhausted and demoralized. The baby was due in less than a month. I had given notice at work and had begun training my replacement. I lived thousands of miles from my family. No one even knew my husband was abusive. At that point, I felt trapped.

Stories in the news about abuse are shocking to those who are unfamiliar with the subject. They might ask, "Why does anyone tolerate that behavior? Why don't they leave?"

It may seem hard to believe that a victim would not run from abuse, especially if it is life threatening. But a victim might stay for one or many of the following reasons.

Careful planning may be needed because safety is a concern when fleeing from abuse. In fact, leaving is often the *most* dangerous time in the relationship, because the abuser is about to lose control and may take drastic measures to keep this from happening. If someone you know is being abused, please encourage the person to call The Hotline to speak with someone experienced in creating a safety plan.

If he/she gives any of the following reasons for staying with an abusive partner please consider offering the following responses:

Reason #1: Denial

The victim of abuse says, "It's not abuse. I have never been hit."

Response:

"There are two things to consider: First, physical abuse is just one of several types of abuse. Other types might seem less serious than physical abuse but they are still very harmful. Second, any abuse can eventually lead to physical abuse even if it hasn't happened yet."

Reason #2: "Love"

The victim says, "But he/she loves me and I love him/her."

Response:

"There are many definitions of love, including self-love. Love does not include intimidation, threats, demeaning and controlling behaviors, or harm. Be sure to love yourself enough to value your own happiness and safety."

Reason #3: Guilt

The victim says, "It's all my fault." The abusive partner may have said that it is the victim's fault so many times that the victim has come to believe it.

Response:

"Abusive people blame their victims rather than admit they are at fault. The victim of abuse is not at fault. The abusive person is at fault."

Reason #4: Pity

The victim says, "That's what he/she learned growing up." The victim takes pity on the abusive person, making excuses by saying that he/she doesn't know any better.

Response:

"Your partner may think abusive behavior is normal and acceptable. But it is unhealthy and unsafe. Measure its impact on your happiness and well-being. What you allow will continue."

Reason #5: The Desire to Rescue

The victim thinks, "I can fix him/her." The victim may truly believe he/she can love the abuse away.

Response:

"We have no power to change others, but we can change ourselves. Your intentions may be kind, but you are risking more harm. If you stay with your abusive partner something worse is likely to happen."

Reason #6: Low Self-Esteem

Abuse can be subtle. Over time, the victim's sense of self-worth can become so worn down that he/she feels the poor treatment is deserved. The victim feels trapped and can't plan an escape. The victim may have doubts about managing alone and may assume he/she won't find anyone better.

Response:

"Call The Hotline. Tell a trusted friend. Get help from a support group. Others know how you feel. People who understand can help you rebuild your self-esteem and your life."

Reason #7: Money

If isolated from family and friends, the victim may have no one to turn to for help with basic expenses. This is especially true if children are involved or if the victim is unemployed. The victim may feel trapped and dependent on the abusive partner's paycheck, health insurance, home, and car.

Response:

"Call The Hotline for help. Safe houses and resources are out there to help you transition from abuse to safety. Find out about them."

Reason #8: Embarrassment and Shame

The embarrassment and shame over the breaking of marital vows, the failure of the relationship, or how his/her reputation might suffer prevent the victim from leaving.

Response:

"It's hard to accept failure but this is not a safe relationship. Non-judgmental support is available to help. Call The Hotline."

Reason #9: Fear

The victim has been warned that if he/she ever attempts to leave, the abusive partner will:

- Harm the victim and/or the children
- Harm himself/herself
- Disappear with the children
- Have the victim deported
- Out the victim if he/she is not ready to share his/her sexual orientation

Response:

"These are legitimate concerns. Careful planning is required for safety. Trained hotline personnel can help you plan a safe escape, consider a U-visa (which provides an opportunity to gain legal status if you cooperate with law enforcement), and address any other concerns. Call The Hotline. They will take threats seriously."

Think twice before following the advice of anyone who downplays the danger you are in—or places the importance of marital vows (or anything else) ahead of your safety—by advising you to stay in an abusive relationship (other than long enough to plan a safe escape).

Leaving an abusive partner will be easier if you can spot abuse and leave right away. But even if the abuse has gone on for some time, you can still become a survivor by using the help available. Be sure to call The Hotline for help in your area. Also use the resources listed at the back of this book.

1-800-799-7233   www.thehotline.org
1-866-331-9474   www.loveisrespect.org

How to Break Up With An Abusive Partner

If you are **living with your abusive partner**, you may need a detailed plan that is customized to your specific situation to break up safely. Your ability to think clearly and make plans—to keep you and your loved ones safe before, during, and after leaving—can be hindered by the crisis. Safety-trained personnel at The Hotline can help you with important details you may not have thought of. They will help you devise a customized, safe plan. Call The Hotline.

If you are **not living together**, plan the breakup very carefully to ensure your safety. Tell a trusted friend or family member what you are planning. Alert them to your chosen time and **public** place.

- Do not break up in private.

- Rehearse what you plan to say.

- Be firm, final, and brief.

- Do not defend your decision because your abuser may try to convince you to stay together.

- Do not announce the breakup on social media.

- Arrange for a trusted friend to "happen by" just as you finish so you are not alone as you leave.

- Do not plan any future private visits with your abusive ex-partner.

Volunteers at The Hotline can also assist with how to tell your family and friends about the abuse and how to take legal action.

1-800-799-7233 www.thehotline.org
1-866-331-9474 www.loveisrespect.org

Being Single

At last! I could feel happiness returning—happiness that had quietly leaked away, little by little, like helium out of a balloon near the floor. I was back in control of my life. Not to say it was easy. There were many challenging moments. I had to regrow confidence in my own judgment. I took safety precautions around my ex-husband. But health insurance had helped with counseling. I had support and encouragement at work. I could see my way forward on a much safer, healthier path. The benefits of being rid of an abusive partner far outweighed any apprehension I might have felt about going it alone.

Although this book is primarily about relationships, there is something to be said for simply being single. Each of us will likely be alone at some time in our lives.

A failed relationship can make you wary of ever attempting another. Being single allows you to re-establish your individual identity. It allows you to get your life back on track. Enjoy the freedom of independence and the confidence that comes with knowing how to enjoy being single.

When you understand and respect yourself, you are a stronger, healthier individual. You are more likely to succeed in a relationship, should you choose one, and less likely to tolerate abuse.

Conclusion

Choose your partner carefully, because the person you choose can impact your well-being well into the future. No one deserves abuse. But the statistics tell us that too often people choose the wrong partner.

By knowing more specifically which healthy behaviors to look for and which unhealthy behaviors to avoid you can make a more informed choice. You can establish boundaries before getting deeply involved. You can recognize abusive behaviors and leave abuse behind, before things become worse.

Safeguard against choosing an unhealthy partner. Before you commit, allow ample time for his/her true nature to surface. If red flags appear in your relationship, don't ignore them. Remember: You cannot fix someone else, *and* abuse usually escalates.

Healthy partnerships are possible, but they don't just happen. They develop between two individuals who truly care about each other, and who are willing to share power, honor each other's boundaries, and earn each other's trust and respect. Remember: love never includes harmful behaviors or danger.

Many people have experienced and survived abuse. Staff members and volunteers who understand this subject are ready to help. If you are a victim of abuse and are ready to become a survivor, or if you simply need more information, call The Hotline.

1-800-799-7233   www.thehotline.org
1-866-331-9474   www.loveisrespect.org

Resources

Statistics about abuse in the United States

from the National Domestic Violence Hotline website:
http://thehotline.org/resources/statistics/

On average, 24 people per minute are victims of rape, physical violence, or stalking by an intimate partner—more than 12 million women and men over the course of a year.

More than 1 in 3 women and more than 1 in 4 men have experienced rape, physical violence, and/or stalking by an intimate partner.

Nearly half of all women and men have experienced psychological aggression by an intimate partner.

Females ages 18 to 34 generally experienced the highest rates of intimate partner violence.

The Hotline History-Milestones

from the National Domestic Violence Hotline website: http://www.thehotline.org/about-us/history/

September 13, 1994—The Violence Against Women Act (VAWA) drafted by then Senator, Joe Biden was signed into law by President Bill Clinton. It authorizes the creation of a NATIONAL DOMESTIC VIOLENCE HOTLINE.

February 21, 1996—The Hotline took its first call.

August 2, 2003—The Hotline took its one-millionth call.

September 26, 2006—Verizon Wireless offered direct connection to The Hotline through the #HOPE initiative – dialing #HOPE from any Verizon Wireless phone instantly connects callers to The Hotline.

February 8, 2007—Liz Claiborne Inc. teamed with The Hotline to launch www.loveisrespect.org, the National Teen Dating Abuse Helpline.

October 21, 2008—The Hotline took its two-millionth call.

September 26, 2011—Love Is Respect announced the nation's first dating abuse texting service.

January 29, 2013—At a special congressional briefing, The Hotline announced they were expecting to take the 3-millionth call nearly one year earlier than predicted highlighting the vital role The Hotline plays.

March 7, 2013—President Obama reauthorized the Violence Against Women Act with provisions that extend the protection to Native American women and members of the LGBT community.

October, 2013—The Hotline launched live chat services, sponsored by Verizon.

July 15, 2015—The Hotline celebrated the grand opening of a new digital services office in Washington, DC.

National Domestic Violence Hotline:

Telephone: 1-800-799-SAFE (7233)

Telephone: 1-800-787-3224 (TTY)

Website: **www.thehotline.org**

Online Chat: 19 hours/day from 7am – 2am Central Time

Call The Hotline or visit the website and learn of other resources in your state and resources specifically designed for certain populations.

National Teen Dating Violence Helpline:

Telephone: 1-866-331-9474

Website: www.loveisrespect.org

Chat: 24/7/365   Text: loveis to 22522

Tech Safety

Please be aware: It is impossible to completely erase search history from your computer. It may be necessary to use a public computer at the local library. Also note that GPS tracking devices can be put in your phone, your car, or your purse. It may be wise to use a different telephone if you think your abuser is monitoring yours. National Domestic Violence Hotline personnel can help you with safety planning. Visit the website for other safety tips: **www.thehotline.org.**

Visit **www.techsafety.org and www.nnedv.org**

(then choose resources, then technology safety) for **technology safety information** involving your computer, tablet, and telephone.

Verizon Wireless **customers can press**

#HOPE from any Verizon Wireless phone to connect to The National Domestic Violence Hotline.

www.whengeorgiasmiled.org has important information about intimate partner violence. The **Aspire News App** was created by Robin McGraw (wife of Dr. Phil). Among other things, this app allows a victim to pre-type a text message or pre-record a voice message to best friends, family members, or 911. It has a GO button you push 3 times to send your message, which alerts your designated contacts to an abusive episode that may happen soon or that you are already in the midst of.

Organizations

National Network to End Domestic Violence
1400 16th St. NW, Suite 330
Washington, D.C. 20036
Telephone: 1-202-543-5566
Website: www.NNEDV.org

National Coalition Against Domestic Violence
One Broadway, Suite B210
Denver, CO 80203
Telephone: 1-303-839-1852
TTY: 1-303-839-1681

Website: www.NCADV.org

NCADV Public Policy Office
2000 M Street, NW, Suite 480
Washington, DC 20036
Telephone: 1-202-467-8714

California Partners to End Domestic Violence
email: **info@cpedv.org**
P.O. Box 1798
Sacramento, CA 95812-1798
Telephone: 1-916-444-7163

Domestic Abuse Intervention Programs
202 East Superior Street
Duluth, MN 55802
Telephone: 1-218-722-2781

Domestic Abuse Project
204 West Franklin Ave.
Minneapolis, MN 55404
Telephone: 1-612-874-7063
email: dap@mndap.org

Futures Without Violence
100 Montgomery Street, The Presidio
San Francisco, CA 94129
Telephone: 1-415-678-5500
TTY: 1-866-678-8901

Institute on Domestic Violence in the African American Community
Website: www.idvaac.org

Alianza National Latino Alliance
for the Elimination of Domestic Violence:
Website: www.dvalianza.org

LGBTQ Domestic Violence Hotline
Telephone: 1-800-832-1901
Website: www.glbtqdvp.org

YWCA Sonoma County
PO Box 3506
Santa Rosa, CA 95402
Hotline: 1-707-546-1234

Other Assistance

The **Safe at Home Program** provides a confidential, free post office box through the CA Secretary of State to allow domestic violence survivors to receive first-class mail, open a bank account, complete confidential name changes, register to vote, enroll their children in school and more without fear of being tracked down by their abusers.

Website: www.sos.ca.gov/registries/safe-home/

California State Victim Compensation reimburses victims for costs related to crimes, such as medical and dental treatment, mental health services, income loss, job retraining, home security, relocation, and crime scene cleanup. Advocates will also help victims find emergency food, clothing, and shelter, file for a temporary restraining order, attend court hearings, and refer them to other services.
Website: www.vcgcb.ca.gov

Health Insurance for Survivors of Abuse
If at any point during the year, a survivor needs to

purchase his/her health insurance, he/she should do the following:

Call the Healthcare.gov Call Center at 1-800-318-2596. (It's important to call rather than apply online, because this is the only way to qualify for a Special Enrollment Period.)

When speaking with the Call Center, be sure to use the phrase "survivor of domestic violence." This will help them initiate the appropriate process.

The Call Center will grant a Special Enrollment Period, and the survivor will have 60 days to pick and enroll in a plan.

Some survivors will be eligible for financial assistance that will make health insurance much more affordable. There are specific rules for survivors who are still married but no longer living with their abuser. When applying, survivors should **mark "unmarried"** on their application so their eligibility determination will be based on their income (and not their spouses'). You don't need documentation to prove domestic violence for the Special Enrollment Period or to receive financial help. But self-attestation is required on tax forms the following year. These policies are for all survivors of domestic violence—both women and men.

Tax Assistance for Survivors of Abuse

There are tax protections for victims under the "Innocent Spouse Relief" program, IRS Publication 971. This publication explains when a spouse may be relieved of tax, interest, and penalties on a joint tax return. Please consult a tax advisor or contact your https://www.irs.gov/publications/p971/. Also, visit the VITA tax site to see if you qualify for free tax preparation: https://www.irs.gov/Individuals/Free-Tax-Return-Preparation-for-You-by-Volunteers

Email the author: info@abuseredflags.com

Sources

1. Domestic Violence Victims & Chronic Health Problems. Available at: http://www.cdc.gov/violenceprevention/intimatepartnerviolence/consequences.html

2. The Adverse Childhood Experiences Study: "What's an ACE Score?" Available at: http://www.acestudy.org/ace_score

3. "Domestic Violence Roundtable: The Effects of Domestic Violence on Children." Available at: http://www.domesticviolenceroundtable.org/effect-on-children.html

4. "Domestic Abuse May Affect Children in Womb." Available at: http://www.msutoday.msu.edu/news/2014/domestic-abuse-may-affect-children-in-womb

5. "Your Amazing Brain: How being in love affects your brain." Available at: www.youramazingbrain.org

6. "Training Institute on Strangulation Prevention: Impact of Strangulation Crimes." Available at: http://www.strangulationtraininginstitute.com/impact-of-strangulation-crimes/

7. "Dr. Lenore Walker: Victim Advocate for Battered Women." Available at: http://www2.webster.edu/~woolflm/walker.html

8. Domesticviolence.org: "The Cycle of Violence." Available at: http://www.domesticviolence.org/cycle-of-violence/

Acknowledgments

I am grateful to the following people for their contributions to this book:

Annie Stuart of Encore Editorial Services for donating her editing expertise.
Telephone: 707-242-6171
Website: www.encoredit.com

LeslieNicolePhotography@yahoo.com

Doug Focht for design help with the cover.

Paula Israel and Misty Bastoni for their learned insights and help with this project.

Lydia Avery, Niki Brunson, Joyce Kerr, Dana Montoro, Earlene Sykes, Jordan Wilson, and Michelle Wing for many helpful suggestions, and especially to Oliver D'Adam for both his helpful suggestions and constant encouragement.

Thank you.

Printed in Great Britain
by Amazon